Cool STEAM Careers

ARCHITECT

SAMANTHA BELL

Published in the United States of America by Cherry Lake Publishing
Ann Arbor, Michigan
www.cherrylakepublishing.com

Content Adviser: Christine Nass, LEED AP, Bachelor of Science in Architecture, University of Michigan, Ann Arbor, MI
Reading Adviser: Marla Conn, ReadAbility, Inc.

Photo Credits: © auremar/Shutterstock Images, cover,1; © EyeMark/Canstock Images, 5; © Phant/Shutterstock
Images, 6; © NG Design/Shutterstock Images, 9; © Goodluz/Shutterstock Images, 10; © Monkey Business Images/
Shutterstock Images, 12; © micheldenijs/iStock Images, 15; © Wavebreakmedia Ltd/Thinkstock Photos, 16;
© JCVstock/Shutterstock Images, 17; © Dragon Images/Shutterstock Images, 18; © ChrisVanLennepPhoto |
Dreamstime.com - Architect Working Computer Designing Photo, 22; © joyfull/Shutterstock.com, 25; © Jlhope |
Dreamstime.com - Solar Energy Building Photo, 26; © racorn/Shutterstock Images, 29

Library of Congress Cataloging-in-Publication Data

Bell, Samantha.
  Architect/Samantha Bell.
    pages cm.—(Cool STEAM careers)
  Includes index.
  ISBN 978-1-63362-554-9 (hardcover)—ISBN 978-1-63362-734-5 (pdf)—ISBN 978-1-63362-644-7 (pbk.)—
ISBN 978-1-63362-824-3 (ebook)
  1. Architects—Juvenile literature. 2. Architecture–Vocational guidance—Juvenile literature. I. Title.

  NA2555.B45 2015
  720.92—dc23
                            2015005328

Cherry Lake Publishing would like to acknowledge the work of
the Partnership for 21st Century Skills. Please visit *www.p21.org*
for more information.

Printed in the United States of America
Corporate Graphics

ABOUT THE AUTHOR

Samantha Bell is a children's book writer, illustrator, teacher, and mom of four busy kids. Her
articles, short stories, and poems have been published online and in print.

TABLE OF CONTENTS

STEAM is the acronym for Science, Technology, Engineering, Arts, and Mathematics. In this book, you will read about how each of these study areas is connected to a career in architecture.

CHAPTER 1

BUILDING FOR CENTURIES

Brian liked looking out the car window on his way to school each day. His favorite building was the new restaurant, which was still under **construction**.

The lot had been empty at first. Then the land was leveled and a foundation was poured. Next, the walls went up. Now the outside of the building was almost finished.

"Someday, I want to build something like that," Brian said to his mom. "But how do the workers know what to do?"

Every building begins with an architect's plan.

"They have an **architect**," Brian's mom answered. "The architect creates the plans for the building. The builders follow the plans."

An architect is a person who plans and oversees a building's construction. Architects may also work on interior details, such as furniture. A building's **design** involves more than its appearance. Buildings must meet the needs of the people who use them. They must be functional, economical, and safe.

The pyramids in Giza, Egypt were built about 4,000

The Colosseum, in Rome, Italy, was built nearly two thousand years ago.

years ago as burial chambers for Egyptian pharaohs. Some people think that one of the pharaoh's advisers, a man named Hemon, was the architect of the Great Pyramid, the largest one. If so, he was one of the world's first architects.

The ancient Greeks and Romans also had architects. They designed temples, theaters, stores, bridges, and **aqueducts**. The Romans introduced arches, using them to build massive structures. Later, during the Middle Ages, **guilds** were formed for different types of craftsmen, including architects. But it wasn't until the Renaissance that individual architects received credit for their designs. Men like Michelangelo and Brunelleschi helped create some of the buildings that have lasted for hundreds of years.

In the 19th century, the first architecture schools were started. Graduates of the schools formed organized societies. Today, architects are creating buildings with both the people and the environment in mind. They must work hard to gain the education, skills, and experience needed to develop these designs.

THINK ABOUT MATH

*Architects must be good at math. Math is required to make many of the decisions about the design and construction of buildings. It is also used to determine key elements in a building's plans, such as the amount of weight a specific wall can support. In addition, architects use math to make good financial decisions and stay within their **budgets**.*

Becoming an Architect

Do you like to draw? Are you good with details?
Do you enjoy a challenge? If so, architecture might be
the career for you. But there are other skills and
qualifications you will need to have as well.

One of the main jobs of an architect is to create the
floor plans of a building. These plans must be clear
enough so **clients** and **contractors** understand the
project. Architects should be able to draw these plans on
paper, as well as create them using computer software.

Many people can imagine what a structure will look

[21ST CENTURY SKILLS LIBRARY]

A floor plan needs to include many details about the building's features.

like as they see it being built. But good architects can visualize it even in the drawing stage. They can picture the finished building before the project has even started.

Architects must give a lot of attention to details. Building plans must show more than just the layout of the building. They also must describe every part of the building, down to how many light switches will be needed. The architect has to be sure that the plans call for just the right sizes and amounts of everything. Too little of something, and construction will be halted. Too much

Architects need to be able to communicate well with their clients.

of something, and money may be wasted.

Architects should have good written and verbal communication skills. They must be able to communicate their vision to both clients and builders. Bigger projects often require huge teams of architects and other construction specialists. The architects must explain their ideas to everyone involved.

Architects must be problem solvers. They constantly face unexpected challenges as projects move along. Each time potential problems arise, the plans may need to be changed.

Before you can become an architect, you must first earn a college degree. It usually takes five years to earn a bachelor's degree in architecture. Students who want to continue their education can go on to earn a master's or doctorate degree in the field.

The second step to becoming an architect is to complete an **internship**. This training program allows a student to work alongside an architect in a firm. Interns might help design part of a project or build a model. They may prepare documents and construction drawings or

To keep their licenses, architects may need to take more college classes even after graduating.

[21ST CENTURY SKILLS LIBRARY]

research building codes. With this hands-on experience, interns can gain the knowledge and skills they need to work on their own someday.

All states in the U.S. require architects to complete the Architect Registration Examination (ARE). There are seven parts to the exam, and they contain multiple-choice questions and "graphic vignettes," which are questions that require completing drawings on the computer. After passing every part, an architect can be licensed by his or her state. Most states also require some type of continuing education to keep a license. This can involve attending conferences, workshops, and college classes.

THINK ABOUT ENGINEERING

Architects should know the basics of structural engineering. This type of engineering focuses on the framework, or "skeleton," of a building. Structural engineers make sure the framework is stable and secure. Architects and engineers work together to design buildings that are safe to use.

ALL IN A DAY'S WORK

Architects often don't get to choose where their creations will be built. It is quite common for a prospective client to come to an architect with an idea in mind and the land for it already purchased. The client probably has a budget in mind, too. It is the architect's job to connect these three factors together. Sometimes this is easy, and sometimes it is not.

The architect begins by listening carefully to the client and then making sketches. Doing this gives both parties a better understanding of what the project may

Architects often need to revise building plans again and again.

involve. Sometimes the sketches are revised many times before the final plan is settled on. A key issue is the budget. Too often, the client has great ideas but does not have enough money to pay for them. The architect must come up with a list of costs for specific items. The client can then decide what to eliminate.

The architect will meet with specialized engineers to work out plans for heating, cooling, water, and electrical systems. These engineers can help make the finished building work more efficiently and be less

The architect might meet with the client to talk about any problems the building might have.

costly to operate. Their suggestions may require changes in the basic plan. The architect will have to discuss the changes with the client. Sometimes, the changes may cost more now but will save money later. If so, the budget may have to be adjusted, too.

Now the architect and the client can meet with the general contractor to go over the plans in detail. The contractor may point out potential problems, and the plans may need to be revised once again. So far, the project has mostly been talk, but that is about to change.

Based on the final plan, materials can start to be ordered, including wood, steel, cement, nails, screws, windows, doors, sinks, toilets, air conditioners, furnaces, carpet, lights—the list may seem endless. Cities around the world have different requirements for buildings that have to be met. In all cases, many permits need to be obtained before construction can begin. These rules,

The construction phase might take a very long time.

Most architects are proud to show off their completed projects.

requirements, and permits help ensure that the completed building will be safe to use.

Much of an architect's workday is often spent in meetings and doing paperwork. But when the project is finally completed, the architect will tour the building to make sure that everything was done correctly and meets the client's needs.

THINK ABOUT ART

Architecture may be the right career choice for someone who is good at art. Architects need to be able to draw, either by hand or on the computer. They communicate their vision to clients and contractors through their drawings. Architects also need a good sense of design. They must decide the best layout and use of the space.

BENEFITS AND DISADVANTAGES

Architecture can be an interesting career choice. Drawing plans, meeting with contractors and clients, looking over documents, and dealing with last-minute details means an architect will have a variety of jobs to do. Because no two projects are exactly the same, even routine tasks may not be boring.

Architecture is a creative field. As architects gain experience, they can become more involved in the creative design of buildings. Most people who choose this career are passionate about it. They feel a strong

Architects need to be able to communicate their ideas clearly.

sense of satisfaction from the projects they've created.

There are also some disadvantages to a career in architecture. It takes a long time and can cost a lot of money to become a licensed architect. A bachelor of architecture degree takes five years to earn. It takes two to four more years to earn a master's degree. Internships last about three years and usually require long hours for low pay. Starting salaries for licensed architects are considered lower than average when compared with other careers that have similar requirements.

Architects often work long hours in their offices.

A career in architecture can be stressful. Architects must find solutions quickly to issues that come up during a project. They are often the ones held responsible if problems develop. Also, architects may not always have work to do. Their jobs depend on a strong economy. If the economy is weak, fewer structures will be built. Fewer architects would be needed, and some may even lose their jobs.

THINK ABOUT TECHNOLOGY

Architects are taking advantage of today's technology. Computer-aided design (CAD) allows architects to create realistic drawings and graphic images. Other programs give architects three-dimensional views of their designs. Some even include animated walk-throughs! Buildings such as the Guggenheim Museum Bilbao in Spain and the Walt Disney Concert Hall in Los Angeles could not have been designed and built without computer models.

TODAY AND TOMORROW

The **recession** that began in 2008 made earning a living difficult for many architects. The recession caused new construction to slow down. From 2009 to 2011, many architects were laid off. They struggled to find work. Some even began working in new fields.

But today, the number of jobs for architects is increasing again. The Bureau of Labor Statistics predicts these opportunities will continue to grow. Employment of architects is expected to increase more than 17 percent from 2012 to 2022, faster than average for all occupations.

Architects will be needed to create plans for new homes, stores, offices, and other structures. New hospitals and health care facilities will have to be designed as well. Architects will also be hired to create new buildings for schools and universities and renovate older ones.

No matter how bad the economy is, new buildings will always need to be built.

Solar panel roofs are one thing used for environmentally sustainable buildings.

As with many other careers, beginning architects might receive low pay. However, their salaries should increase as they gain more experience. Another factor that can affect salary is the architect's education. Architects with a master's or doctorate degree may earn more than those with only a bachelor's degree.

Geographic location can also have an effect on how much money an architect makes. For example, some of the best-paid architects work in areas like Bridgeport, Connecticut, and Santa Cruz, California.

THINK ABOUT SCIENCE

*Some architects specialize in **green design**, also known as sustainable design. These architects think about the environment when they design a structure. They find ways to conserve energy and water and to reduce pollution. Their plans call for materials that won't harm the environment.*

In 2013, the median annual salary for architects was $74,110. This means that half of the working architects made more money and half of them made less. Architects with the lowest salaries made about $45,000 per year. Those with the highest pay made approximately $119,370 per year.

Architects design the structures people need—houses, offices, airports, schools, churches, hospitals, libraries, shops, and even prisons. If you are imaginative, artistic, and mathematical, a career in architecture might just be the right choice for you. You could be designing the buildings of the future!

Being a successful architect requires a variety of skills.

THINK ABOUT IT

Try to find a teacher, relative, or other adult who is the original owner of the house where they live. Did they talk to an architect to have it designed a certain way? What was that process like? Were there any problems along the way? What parts of their house are they happiest about now?

Walk around your home and take notes on the layout of the rooms. Notice the paths you take to walk from one room to another. Is there an area you think could have been designed a better way? Walk around a friend's home and take notes. How are your living spaces similar? How are they different?

Look nearby where you live for a building that is under construction. Take photos of it. Try to go back every so often to take photos of the building as more progress is made. When the building is completed, compare your photos. What things do you notice? What does this teach you about architecture?

LEARN MORE

FURTHER READING

Beck, Barbara. *The Future Architect's Handbook.* Atglen, PA: Schiffer Publishing, Ltd., 2014.

Dillon, Patrick. *The Story of Buildings: From the Pyramids to the Sydney Opera House and Beyond.* New York: Candlewick, 2014.

Roeder, Annette. *13 Buildings Children Should Know.* New York: Prestel Publishing, 2009.

Salvadori, Mario. *The Art of Construction: Projects and Principles for Beginning Engineers and Architects.* Chicago: Chicago Review Press, 2000.

WEB SITES

Architect of the Capitol
www.aoc.gov
Read about the renovations happening on Capitol Hill in Washington, D.C.

Building Big: Wonders of the World Databank
www.pbs.org/wgbh/buildingbig/wonder/index.html
Play with this cool search engine to find information about the structures that are "wonders of the world."

Dr. Mike's Math Games for Kids: The Math Architect Game
www.dr-mikes-math-games-for-kids.com/math-architect-game.html
Try this fun game where you design apartment blueprints using your knowledge of square roots.

GLOSSARY

aqueducts (AK-wuh-duhkts) structures that carry a large amount of flowing water

architect (AHR-ki-tekt) person who plans, designs, and oversees a building's construction

budgets (BUHJ-its) the amounts of money available for certain purposes

clients (KLYE-uhnts) customers

construction (kuhn-STRUHK-shuhn) process of erecting a building

contractors (KAHN-trakt-urz) people responsible for the day-to-day activities on construction sites

design (dih-ZINE) artistic plan or pattern

floor plans (FLOR PLANZ) diagrams of the arrangement of rooms in a building

green design (GREEN dih-ZINE) design that emphasizes the efficient use of resources

guilds (GILDZ) associations of people with the same interests

internship (IN-turn-ship) a low-paying job in a special field that an advanced student or graduate can work at to get more experience while being supervised by a professional

recession (rih-SESH-uhn) a downward turn in business activity

INDEX